THE SIGN OF JONAH

By Guenter Rutenborn

The Word Was God: *Book by Book Through The Book of Books.* 1959

THE SIGN OF JONAH

JONAH

A Play in Nine Scenes

BY

GUENTER RUTENBORN

Translated from the German by
GEORGE WHITE

THOMAS NELSON AND SONS

Edinburgh   NEW YORK   *Toronto*

. . . he began to say, "This generation is an evil generation; it seeks a sign, but no sign shall be given to it except the sign of Jonah. For as Jonah became a sign to the men of Nineveh, so will the Son of man be to this generation. The queen of the South will arise at the judgment with the men of this generation and condemn them; for she came from the ends of the earth to hear the wisdom of Solomon, and behold, something greater than Solomon is here. The men of Nineveh will arise at the judgment with this generation and condemn it; for they repented at the preaching of Jonah, and behold, something greater than Jonah is here."

Luke 11.29–32, RSVB

CAST OF CHARACTERS
(*in order of appearance*)

THE JUDGE

JONAH, THE PROPHET

A MAN IN THE AUDIENCE

MERCHANT

GABRIEL ⎫
MICHAEL ⎬ ARCHANGELS
RAPHAEL ⎭

THE AVERAGE MAN

THE QUEEN OF THE SOUTH, BABYLON, NINEVEH

THE AVERAGE WOMAN

STAGE MANAGER

The action is set in a theatre in West Berlin.

The time is now.

The curtain rises. The stage is in complete darkness while the houselights are still on. When the house-lights finally dim, we can make out Jonah and the Judge sitting on the bench to the right of center stage, talking to each other as if unaware that the curtain is up.

In the very center of the stage is a sort of pulpit which also serves as the Judge's bench. Otherwise the stage is bare. Elaborate costumes are not required. Jonah is dressed in yellow oilcloth, a rain-coat and sweater. The Judge and, later, the Arch-angels wear long robes of rather somber colors, and the upper part of their faces are masked. Whenever the characters step out of their historical parts, they remove their masks and are thus recognizable as our contemporaries. Only the Queen is dressed ac-cording to the Revelation to John, 17.4.

SCENE ONE

JUDGE

What do you mean, you don't want to?

JONAH

There's no point to it.

JUDGE

The audience is here, the performance must go on as scheduled. You just can't decide at the last moment. . . .

JONAH

Of course I can. I don't want to. I just don't want to.

JUDGE

Aha! Exactly like the biblical Jonah. He didn't want to, either.

JONAH

Precisely unlike the biblical Jonah. He, at least, *was* successful. He *was* able to convert a great city.

11

JUDGE

Yet he did it reluctantly; he wasn't at all pleased that Nineveh became converted.

JONAH

And I'm not pleased that the people today refuse to become converted. The world has been turned upside down, everything is completely topsy-turvy, only the people haven't changed. Everything has remained the same.

JUDGE

The more reason for us to perform tonight.

JONAH

Perform? Before whom? Do you really think we have the right audience?

JUDGE

Signs do occur. They don't necessarily depend upon an audience.

JONAH

O, the public has changed. Yes, when our cities were heaps of rubble the people seemed different. But now that the cities are almost entirely rebuilt, do you think they still remember—or even want to be reminded of those days when fire and destruction rained from the skies? Today, wherever you look, you only see those damn neon lights.

JUDGE

Even now, sometimes, when clearing away left-over debris they find duds. . . .

JONAH

Duds! O yes, duds! Then there's a big commotion, lots of excitement, talk. The police rope off the area, the entire neighborhood is evacuated. But when human remains are discovered among the rubble it is removed in the dark of night. Secretly. So no one will be offended. No! Nowadays we're far too concerned with the living, and not at all with the dead. Life today is far too noisy for my taste. Too many cars, portable radios, portable TVs. But the dead for whom I'm supposed to speak here tonight—are silent. Silent and helpless.

JUDGE

I don't believe that. Let me tell you something. No, the people haven't forgotten. Listen. In 1954, in December, I went to London, to root for our National Team in the soccer match against England. On the trip back, near Louvain, the engine jumped the tracks, rolled down the embankment and pulled along the first three cars. I was in one.

JONAH

You? You were in that wreck?

JUDGE

Well, yes. But it isn't the accident itself I want to talk about.

JONAH

It must have been horrible.

JUDGE

Not worse than what happened to you in that submarine. No, I shouldn't even mention both in one breath. You were the sole survivor. I was one of about twenty. . . .

JONAH

Twenty? Only . . . about twenty? Not more?

JUDGE

Well, forgive me for using the blunt language of men who've survived disaster. Yes, one of about twenty. But as I said before, it isn't the accident I want to talk about. What I do want you to know is what happened when we arrived in Aachen. There was a big crowd waiting, journalists, reporters. One of the reporters, he was from the North-German Broadcasting Company—strange, isn't it, that such unimportant details cling to your mind?—was utterly amazed at the way we expressed ourselves when he asked us if there had been a panic, whether the people had been very frightened. . . .

JONAH

Which car did you say you were in?

JUDGE

The third. It rolled down the embankment and crashed on top of the second.

JONAH

Horrible.

JUDGE

Well, yes. But to get back to the reporter. He almost re-
fused to believe us when we told him that the passengers
remained completely calm.

JONAH

Calm?! Why, that's incredible!

JUDGE

But true. I often wondered about it until much later a
psychologist explained it to me. We were able to remain
calm, he said, because we had been conditioned by our experiences during the war. So you see, the memories have
remained alive. Very much alive, in spite of neon lights and
the enthusiasm for soccer. I've no doubt that the audience
still remembers. So go ahead, start the play!

JONAH

            (Turning around and pretending to see audience
            for first time)
Which, of course, we've already done, Ladies and Gentlemen.

JUDGE

            (Also facing audience)
The bit with the open curtain was the first trick.

JONAH

The first trick. Yes. The first of several.
> (In the audience a man rises most indignantly)

MAN IN THE AUDIENCE

Trick! I always hear "trick." What is this? A circus? I was under the impression I would see a serious play, a biblical play. That's what you advertised in the papers, didn't you? Well, that's why I'm here. But "trick, trick!" I'm leaving. I want my money back. . . .

JUDGE

You are seeing a biblical play. Please . . . ! Why don't you stay, Mister. . . .

MAN IN THE AUDIENCE

Trick. My name's Trick.

JUDGE

Ah, Mister Trick. A pleasure, indeed a pleasure. All right then, to begin.
> (Pointing at JONAH)

This is Jonah. You've heard of Jonah, haven't you? Jonah, one of the minor prophets.

MAN IN THE AUDIENCE

Jonah? O yes. Isn't he the one who allegedly was swallowed by a whale?

JUDGE

JUDGE

Yes, absolutely correct. The one from the Bible, who later
went to Nineveh to preach about death and resurrection.
Perhaps you're familiar with the story.

MAN IN THE AUDIENCE

Yes, yes, I seem to remember now. Not too clearly though.

JUDGE

Well, that's forgivable. It happened a very long time ago,
and such things are difficult to substantiate. This sort of
submersion went unreported in the press. But our Jonah,
as you've just heard, immersed himself not only in the prob-
lems of our age but also in prophecy.
　　　(Gesturing to JONAH)
Jonah, if you please.
　　　　　(JUDGE exits and the curtain falls, but JONAH has
　　　　　stepped in front of it, and very casually sits down
　　　　　on the edge of the proscenium)

JONAH

Yes, I'm Jonah. The Jonah who was swallowed by a whale. Well, actually, this is what really happened. During the last war, when I was in command of a submarine. . . .

MAN IN THE AUDIENCE

Submarine! I was led to believe you're the Prophet Jonah.

MERCHANT

(Sitting in the back of the audience calls out)
Quiet up front!

JONAH

It's imperative only for a man to identify himself with a fact, with a certain matter, with an occurrence. Let me explain. Well, as I said before, during the Second World War I was in command of a submarine. We were cruising on the surface when suddenly we were attacked by a bomber; we had to crash dive. Something went wrong. We hit bottom. We couldn't move. We were stuck. Needless to say, the engineer tried everything possible; it was of no avail. We were doomed to the slow death of suffocation. I venture to say that suffocation is the most horrible form of death—but then, I suppose, one's own death usually is the most horrible. "What's going to happen to us?" the crew kept asking over and over again, a little more desperate each time. "You'll die!" I finally shouted angrily. "To die is part of your job!" The engineer sneered, "Why not try prayers?" "We'd rather curse," the men shouted back. And curse they did. I don't suppose I have to tell you how adept sailors are at cursing. But after a while even the cursing stopped, for strange as it may seem, no one can go on cursing indefinitely. "Now only a miracle can pry us loose," said the engineer. He said many more things, and then he began to cry, very softly. Tears are catching. Soon others were crying too. But again, there's no need to go into details. Suffice it to say that on the average, they were rather young lads, and they cried for their dear ones. As for myself, I was rather apathetic. When they kept asking me how I felt, I became annoyed and shouted, "I'm praying!" It wasn't the truth. Well, before long, the thing I had dreaded most did happen. One of the men committed suicide. The engineer. Everyone panicked. I suppose that's only natural. There is something horrifying about sharing a stifling hot tinfish with a corpse. We were also beginning to feel the lack of oxygen. If you further keep in mind the slow, monotonous fashion in which time passed, then you'll understand that before long I had to cope with a virtual epidemic of suicides. I was powerless. I couldn't be everywhere at once, and furthermore, the lack of oxygen made rapid movement imprudent. At long last there were only two of us left. By a strange coincidence the other man's name was Abel, Abel Moeller.

Abel, by the way, is a Hebrew name. Well, Abel had discovered one last oxygen tank just as we thought the end
had come. "I'm going to live," he shouted excitedly. A most
foolish thing to do, getting excited when there's so precious
little oxygen. I tried my best to calm him down. "Easy, son,
easy," I said, but Abel had reached for a revolver and was
aiming at me. The pistol jammed. He began to sob and
threw himself into my arms and begged for forgiveness. "All
right," I told him, "release the oxygen. We'll see who'll
suffocate first. God, in whom neither of us believes, shall
be our judge!" We sat down next to each other. He was
crying and I—I suddenly found the strength to pray. I
prayed very quietly, very calmly. You can guess why. Right!
To make the oxygen last a little longer. Then the sobbing
next to me began to peter out. Suddenly Abel flung out his
arms in a violent spasm, his skin turned dark, almost purple
. . . no, I'd just as soon spare you the gory details. God
had judged him and taken no heed of his tears of remorse.
I fell to my knees and in a choking voice I vowed, "If you'll
let me survive I shall become Your witness!"—Then I tried
the valves once again—you know, the valves that regulate
the pressurized air that forces water out of the diving chambers. "In the name of the Lord," I shouted, "flee, you evil
spirits of the deep!" I heard a vicious, angry hissing—yes,
vicious and angry! But to me it sounded like a chorus of
angels' voices!

        (He now stands up)

Well, as you can see, I'm here, and now I call myself Jonah.
And why not? Whether submarine or whale, hell is always
one and the same. As a matter of fact, much, very much,

always remains one and the same. Jonah tells the venerable, somewhat juvenile tale that he had gone to Nineveh to preach about death and resurrection. Nineveh! Why Nineveh? After all today, this evening, we are in Berlin. In our playlet, even while the performance goes on, Nineveh becomes Babylon, by which Saint John, whose Revelations are our source, meant Rome. Yes, one must know the original texts. It is important to know the original texts. And what is in a name? Does the name really matter? Nineveh, Berlin, Babylon, Rome . . . tomorrow it might be New York, Moscow . . . who knows. Ah, but the original texts! Take this quotation, for example: mene, mene, tekel upharsin.

       (He pretends to notice that the audience does not
          undersand the meaning of the saying)

I beg your pardon? O, you're not familiar with that quotation. A pity. A real pity!

       (Pointing at audience)

And you're the ones to be pitied. One should have understood its meaning long ago—after all, at one time it was a commonly used expression in Germany. The original menetekel—that too, by the way, is Hebrew—was written in fiery letters into the walls of Belshazzar's banquet hall, just, as a lot more recently, it was written across the width and breadth of our country. It means—and hasn't it truly come to pass?—it means numbered, numbered, weighed and divided. If you're interested in the full story you can read it in the book written by my colleague Daniel. But we had better stick with Jonah, with the Prophet Jonah, with the Sign of Jonah!

       (He snaps his fingers, to indicate that the curtain
          is to be raised and also that the lights are to go on.)

SCENE
THREE

(The JUDGE enters again, followed by the Archangels GABRIEL, MICHAEL and RAPHAEL)

JUDGE

I have agreed to enact the part of the Judge. According to
latest research there exists, besides the Archangels . . .
(Pointing at them)
these three gentlemen, here . . . a well substantiated, old
tradition of an angel who sits in Judgment. I have agreed
to enact that part since I had ample opportunity to get to
know a large segment of our present-day nations. I was in
Italy—in uniform, not as a tourist—then in North Africa.
Oh yes, I became well acquainted with the charming
Italians and the honorable Africans—and I learned to re-
spect the British. Close to the end of the war I fell into
French captivity. The French! I learned to hate them! Yes,
hate them as passionately as I had once loved and revered
them. Then I was turned over to the Russians. At first I
hated the Russians, but soon they persuaded me to love
them. As for the Germans whom I had loved all my life, I
learned to hold them in deepest contempt, because. . . .

JONAH

(Stepping toward him)
Enough, already! Enough! We're not concerned with your private life and opinions. You're the Judge. We expect you to be severe, but impartial. It is your duty to weigh all nations according to one inflexible standard of justice.

GABRIEL

I'm supposed to represent the Archangel Gabriel. Gabriel means "God is my strength." I'm here neither as the sole survivor from a U-boat, nor as a repatriate from Siberia. But I was in Dresden when the Yanks paid us a flying visit. Buried alive in a basement for ten days I was. Has anyone of you experienced Dresden?
(He pauses for a moment)
Let me tell you it was deliberate murder. Dastardly murder.

JONAH

Quiet! Quiet! The part of the Judge is not played by you but by Mister . . .
(He gives the real name of actor playing JUDGE.
Then, to audience)
Well, he's also a survivor.

MICHAEL

And my name is Michael. Translated that means, "Who is like God?" A question like that shouldn't really be asked, should it? You're bound to get a stupid answer. You know what I mean, don't you?
(He gives the Hitler salute)

As for myself, well, the Amis interned me at the Dachau
concentration camp. Yes, you heard right, the Amis, the
Americans. They beat us and kept us on a near-starvation
diet. Me, me of all people. For this nonsense . . .
        (He gives Hitler salute)
was something for which for a long time already I felt
nothing but contempt. As a matter of fact, that was the
reason I wound up with a penal company assigned to carry
out mass executions in the East. But only of inferior races.
Well, don't think for a moment it was a pleasant job we
had. . . .

JONAH

        (To audience)
Another survivor!
        (To RAPHAEL)
Next, please.

RAPHAEL

My name is Raphael. It means simply—if you'll pardon the
expression—"Heil God!"

JONAH

Another survivor, without doubt.

RAPHAEL

You bet. Escaped from East Prussia, crossed the Baltic on
a small fishing vessel, bombed, strafed. . . .

GABRIEL

You're tugging at my heart strings. Ah, cut it out! Are you
trying to impress me, a veteran of Dresden?

RAPHAEL

Afterwards, somewhere in Pomerania, I was stood up against a wall . . . and executed.

MICHAEL

What?

RAPHAEL

They missed, natch! They were stinking drunk, otherwise I'd be a real angel by now.

JONAH

(Shaking his head doubtfully and amusedly)
Well, well, well. . . .

MICHAEL

I've been saying it all along: we're not angels.

JONAH

Yes, it is rather indisputable that we Germans never had any excessive relations with angels; rather with the opposite number.

RAPHAEL

See Goethe's *Faust!*

MICHAEL

And Thomas Mann's *Doctor Faustus.*

JONAH

All right, all right; let's get started.

RAPHAEL

(Coming to the center, he recites)
The sonorous sun, in ancient fashion
In song match joins the brother spheres. . . .

JONAH

Hey! Not that! Cut it out!
(Contemptuously)
Classicist!

RAPHAEL

I merely wanted to prove that there are angels in *Faust*.

JONAH

Cut out the gibberish. Get down to business. Begin.

RAPHAEL

Begin? Where?

JONAH

At the conclusion.
(When RAPHAEL pretends not to understand, the
JUDGE steps into the center)

JUDGE

With Judgment Day. For Judgment Day is at hand. The
destruction of Babylon, alias Rome, alias Dresden, alias Ber-

lin, alias Coventry, alias Rotterdam, alias Hiroshima, alias Nagasaki, et cetera, et cetera, proves it. The spirits of the lower depths have risen, the Atom bombs are ready. . . .

RAPHAEL

And the H-bombs. . . .

GABRIEL

And Cobalt bombs. . . .

JONAH

(Teasingly)
Mustn't forget the flying saucers. Anything else?

JUDGE

Stick to the issue at hand, please!
            (He takes his position behind his desk. To the
            audience)
We request your presence on Judgment Day. Trumpets please!
            (Trumpets play a fanfare)
The Court in the Sign of Jonah is now in session!
            (Everyone takes his place, the Archangels come to
            center stage, JONAH, somewhat watchful, always
            ready to comment or interrupt, remains slightly
            to right)

MICHAEL [*]

The day of Judgment dawns
    [*] Poem adapted by Nancy Walker.

And thus the Lord commands his will:
Now let the sun stand still
As once it stood for Joshua
In the Valley of Ajalon.
Let purity in its own bright light,
Like a grand prophetic vision, shimmer,
The day shall never change again to night.

GABRIEL

When the lower depths belched smoke
To stay the newly risen day,
When flames of Hell turned night
Into a blinding noon,
Then was the abyss opened—
The final change evoked;
Then came destruction
In which God's own work must end.

RAPHAEL

Come closer then, you purest works of God.
Give all your beauty to this one great day.
The black abyss in you shall be eclipsed,
And suffering, and all the earth's dismay
Shall come in time to face
The one eternal light.

ALL THREE ARCHANGELS

And so we praise Thee for this very terror's sake.
Hell's fury rages—dies,
Here ends a world in tears.
And after all its cries of pain

Have faded,
That last day's sun will rise.

MICHAEL

Babylon is fallen,
And with it pomp and blasphemy.
Babylon is fallen!
Earth need no longer serve in hate,
The curse is broken and the night takes flight.

GABRIEL

The world has not been shattered
The sighs on sinful lips will praise Him still.
On Babel's black parched walls that burned,
Still rest the shadows of God's strength.

RAPHAEL

Let even those who fall kneel yet again to pray
And know
That God's unbounded beauty can stay the threat of death.
And from this certainty, this new found truth,
Shall they, the fallen, find new hope.

ALL THREE ARCHANGELS

You, who counted time in solemn circles,
Now laud the justice of the universe.
You are the world's order and its ornament
Let God's house tremble with your song.
In you shall the fallen see
That in God's hand lie death and resurrection.

JONAH

Nicely said, gentlemen, very nicely indeed. We are indebted to you. But you did say your piece "sub specie aeternitatis," and it is rather doubtful if anyone in these hectic times can permit himself the luxury of accepting the long-range view, the point of view of eternity.

> (The QUEEN OF BABYLON, the AVERAGE MAN, the AVERAGE WOMAN are coming down the aisle, obviously in answer to the ARCHANGELS' invitation)

Ah, here are three people who have accepted your invitation.

> (Aside to the JUDGE)

Well, we'll see who's right.

> (The QUEEN OF BABYLON, the AVERAGE MAN and the AVERAGE WOMAN have come on stage)

JUDGE

(To JONAH)

You seem to be ill qualified for the legal profession. You merely look at people and immediately form prejudices. Snap judgments. Very bad. I recall having read somewhere that you practiced law in Nineveh without ever arriving at a proper verdict. Snap judgments, prejudices. We shall have to reexamine these cases.

JONAH

What do you mean prejudices? You completely fail to appreciate prophetic insight. Just take an unhurried look at these three. Look at their faces. They are faces from the twentieth century—certainly one of the strangest of all centuries. Well, is there another more weighted down with guilt and blood, and at the same time filled with excuses and self-justifications? The face of twentieth-century man! Hmmm! You can pick out that face from all the faces of all the centuries that have been. Only rarely will you find, combined in one face, so much cruelty, self-righteousness and emptiness, while at the same time it is devoid of all religious feelings. I'm willing to bet that none of those three have the slightest notion where they are. . . .

JUDGE

You're forgetting yourself, prophet.

JONAH

Who can't forget himself must never become a prophet.

JUDGE

Nevertheless we must adhere to an orderly legal procedure.
(To the newcomers)
We are in your debt for accepting our solemn invitation. The court has decided to simplify proceedings by reducing the innumerable counts of the indictment to one special case. The Court requests you hold yourselves available as witnesses.

AVERAGE MAN

Witness? Witness my foot. I'm here as a plaintiff!

JONAH

(To JUDGE)
You see! I've been saying it all along.

JUDGE

(To AVERAGE MAN)
You're entitled to voice your complaints within the framework of your testimony as a witness, provided of course you pay strict attention to truth and objectivity.
(To everyone, dryly)

All right then! Disregarding the numerous inexcusable
crimes committed in the City of Nineveh, alias Babylon or
Babel, alias Rome I, II, III, et cetera, et cetera, the Court
will confine its examinations to the initial case of guilt of
the City, respectively its inhabitants and government. We
shall consider the well-known, precedent-setting, political
case of the three men cast alive into the furnace of fire. See
exhibit one, the Book of Daniel, Chapter Three. It is a
reasonable assumption that our witnesses are familiar with
the matter, since at least one billion copies of the Bible
have been printed in a thousand or so languages and dia-
lects.

(To the QUEEN)
Just in case it has slipped your mind, my dear lady, I will
summarize the facts once again. In the year 602 before
Christ—*before* Christ, though I must emphasize most em-
phatically that this is not to be construed as a mitigating
circumstance—well, in that year 602 an incident occurred
in your city which must be considered the origin of the mis-
fortune which brought about the complete destruction of
your city, the capital of the world, through the fires of hell.
You were responsible for the construction of a furnace into
which were cast alive three respected and well-liked men,
to wit, the Witnesses Shadrach, Meshach and Abednego.
This is a crime against humanity.

RAPHAEL

Correction, Your Honor. Though the three gentlemen were
indeed cast into the furnace of flaming fire, I was sent to
protect them from serious bodily harm. They survived the

ordeal and later were appointed to high administrative offices.

QUEEN

But this incident did not occur during my reign. The power-drunk Nebuchadnezzar gave the order.

JUDGE

What the blazes! What sort of excuse is that? My dear lady, in another minute you shall be properly identified. In his Revelations Saint John supplies us with your criminal warrant.

(To MICHAEL)

Michael, please read the warrant to the Court.

MICHAEL

(Reading from a book)

The word of the Lord: "The woman was dressed in purple and scarlet, and glittered with gold, precious stones, and pearls. She had in her hand a gold cup . . ."

QUEEN

The cup! O, I left it home. It was too much of a bother . . .

AVERAGE MAN

What a dope! Now you've given yourself away.

JONAH

Yes, sweetheart, that wasn't very clever.

JUDGE

And that gold cup contains the very proof. For it was full
of . . . full of . . . Michael!

MICHAEL

"Full of accursed things, and the impurities of her immorality and drunkenness." By the way, by drunkenness is
meant, "drunk with the blood of God's people."

JUDGE

(To the QUEEN)
Well, there's the proof! Or perhaps you cling to the belief
that burning alive is not bloodshed?
(To the audience)
Ladies and Gentlemen, there is one point you all must be
absolutely clear about. This Court is more precise than is
customary in the court of law, even if our methods of inquiry into the mythological and original precedent might
seem somewhat unusual. However, this Court will at no
time tolerate a de-mythologizing, or any other excuses, or
claims of misunderstandings.

JONAH

Hear! Hear!

JUDGE

The Court is not afflicted with a "Psychology of the Super-
ficial." The Court knows precisely the standards it must
adhere to.
(To the QUEEN)

You, Madame, have agreed to enact tonight the part of the
Queen. At another time you're Medea, or Portia, or Mar-
garet. Actually there's no need for these disguises, no one
is fooled. We know exactly who is hiding behind all these
masks. Whether you're enacting the Queen of Babylon or,
on the other hand, the Queen of the South, we know that
in reality you're Miss. . . .

> (He names the real name of actress playing
> QUEEN)

QUEEN

Mister. . . .

> (She names the real name of actor playing JUDGE)
Have you suddenly gone mad? I thought we're playing. . . .

JUDGE

Playing? You're *playing*? I reject the term, playing. I reject
it most adamantly. We judge. We sit in judgment over our
age, and after all, you are a woman of the twentieth century!

QUEEN

Yes.

JUDGE

You agreed to enact the part of the Queen?

QUEEN

What else would I be doing here?

JUDGE

Your insolence makes it absolutely impossible to give favorable consideration to your protests. Now then! To create a character on stage demands a complete identification with that character, doesn't it? The more complete, the better.

JONAH

Friends, let's not waste time with such trivia. Otherwise we'll lay an egg tonight and the author will get blamed.

JUDGE

(To JONAH)
The Court doesn't think the author matters right now. What does matter is that we clarify this point.
(To QUEEN)
Now, Miss. . . .
(He names her real name)
since you are able to identify yourself with such a character as the Queen of Babylon, it follows that you, as a woman of the twentieth century, are capable to *be* that bloodthirsty queen. After all, if you can't identify yourself with the queen you'll present an absolutely implausible, unconvincing character tonight. Correct?

QUEEN

O, this is a horrible play.

JUDGE

You're not to judge the play. That privilege is reserved for the audience and the reviewers. All that is expected of you is a creditable performance.

GABRIEL

(To QUEEN)
I can't see why you're getting all hepped up, Miss . . .
       (He names her real name)
All right, at the suggestion of Guenther Rutenborn we're
concerned with the old story of the three men and the
furnace of fire. Well? Didn't we have furnaces of fire?
Didn't we cast innocent people into the flames? Everyone
knows we did.

JONAH

That is also my contention. The translation of the Hebrew
text into German makes for an interesting parallel.

MICHAEL

It has also been translated into every other language.

RAPHAEL

You certainly find furnaces of fire elsewhere.

JUDGE

We're not concerned with that. We're dealing with the
Hebrew-German precedent alone. By examining the case of
the three men and the furnace of fire in an incendiary
Babylon—or whatever the name might be—we will be forced
to consider other burnt out cities and their incendiaries—
the original incendiaries, if you please. Let us proceed with
the investigation.
             (The AVERAGE WOMAN has been trying to catch
             JUDGE's attention, now she does)
Yes!

AVERAGE WOMAN

Your Honor, please, may I have the floor, Your Honor! I'm what's usually called just an average housewife. You know what I mean. But I like to think that now I'm speaking for all the mothers. Yes, the mothers! Unsung heroines they are, the mothers, suffering the agonies of giving birth, and raising their children with love and worry and fear, only to have a cruel world take them away. Shadrach, Meshach and Abednego! They're my sons! Even today I remember how they promised to fulfill our great hopes in them. O, it wasn't easy, raising them. Just think, Your Honor, three boys at one time. They. . . .

JUDGE

All right, my good woman, all right. Please, confine yourself to answering questions. Do you happen to know how it came about that your sons were arrested and condemned to suffer such a terrible fate?

AVERAGE WOMAN

Do I know! Of course I know! Don't these things always happen the same way? Someone denounced them. You see, Your Honor, there was this decree. And everyone was supposed to obey it. It said, everyone must salute a golden idol, and the standards and the flags. But my boys were intellectuals. It wasn't easy, Your Honor, we had to sacrifice a great deal, but I insisted the boys get a fine education.

JONAH

Well, Mom, now don't you get carried away. The Hebrew original is just a little bit different.

(To MICHAEL)

Perhaps you can help us out once again, Michael.

(MICHAEL opens his book)

MICHAEL

"Thereupon certain Chaldeans came forward and laid an accusation against the Jews, saying to King Nebuchadnazzi —Nebuchadnezzar I meant to say.

(Giving the Hitler salute)

O King, may you live forever—at least a thousand years. You, O King, have made a decree that every man who hears the sound of the horn, the pipe, the lyre, and every other kind of musical instrument, shall fall down and prostrate himself before the image of gold; and whosoever does not fall down and prostrate himself shall be cast into the midst of a furnace of flaming fire. Now, there are certain Jews. . . ."

JUDGE

That'll do. Thank you. The parallel has been clearly established.

(To the AVERAGE WOMAN)

All right, then. Who denounced your sons?

AVERAGE WOMAN

The Queen's already implicated. But she's merely the highest authority.

> (She continues to look around unhurriedly, peer-
> ing into the audience, repeating over and over
> again)

Is there anyone who at one time or another hasn't stooped
to denunciation at least once?

> (Now she is looking straight at MICHAEL, who
> ducks)

MICHAEL

What are you looking at me for? I didn't do it!

JONAH

Now don't get upset. You're supposed to behave like an
angel.

MICHAEL

But Mister. . . .
> (Giving JONAH's real name)
You know I'm not an angel.

JONAH

Well, there's no doubt about that. After all, you're a human
being, and certainly guilty of some minor human transgressions.

MICHAEL

Minor . . . O, I'm not talking about minor transgressions.
It's not that harmless. Before they drafted me into the
Wehrmacht I was a clerk in the municipal marriage license
bureau. I can't help thinking about it . . . often at night
I wake up in a sweat. . . . ! Must I really tell everything?

(His sudden outburst has aroused the JUDGE's curiosity)

JUDGE

You most certainly must. This is Judgment Day. Acquit yourself!

MICHAEL

(He deliberates for a while; then, compelled)
It's a long story; it goes all the way back to the end of the First World War. That Versailles peace treaty got my goat. It was wrong, it deprived me of my West-Prussian home. When Hitler came along and denounced Versailles, I joined the party. In due time I became a clerk in the marriage license bureau. I officiated at weddings and inspected the documents, the birth certificates—well, I suppose you remember why: because of the Aryan grandmothers. I had to certify that all these people had the proper racial background. Well, at first I saw no harm in differentiating between Germans and Jews. But then, later, they built the furnaces. To my great shame—to my eternal shame!—I also consigned people to the furnaces. Yes, yes, I did! I'm a murderer, can't you see! A murderer! A murderer, not an angel!

JONAH

Come, come, man, get hold of yourself. Look. . . .

JUDGE

You're stepping out of character, Mister. . . .
(Giving MICHAEL's real name)

JONAH

Really, my good man, really you're going too far. Just pause
and think for a moment. Consider the implications of your
statement. Think of the innumerable certificates of baptism
issued by Christian clergymen, by municipal clerks.

QUEEN

(Horrified)
O . . . ! Even the author of this play. . . .

JONAH

Yes! Himself a pastor!
(During this entire exchange the AVERAGE WOMAN
has been walking around the stage, looking at the
actors, and then she has gone down into the audience. Now, back on stage again, she stops abruptly
in front of the AVERAGE MAN)

AVERAGE WOMAN

(Screaming)
Now I know! He's the one! He did it!
(To AVERAGE MAN)
You denounced them!

AVERAGE MAN

Ah, you're off your rocker. Lay off me, will you! I'm just
an average man.

AVERAGE WOMAN

Don't you raise your voice. You denounced my boys. You!
You! Who snapped to attention, mornings, noon and night?
Who permitted them to put a uniform on you? Who came
at dawn and knocked at the doors of frightened people?
Who drove the police cars? Guarded the prisons? Was the
executioner? Who? Who built the furnaces? Stoked them?
Who helps tyrants everywhere be tyrants? Who sells his
eyes and ears for a reward? Who builds a monument to
evil?

ALL ON STAGE

(Excepting JUDGE and JONAH)
The Average Man! The Average Man!

JUDGE

(To the AVERAGE MAN)
Ah! So we've finally caught up with you! How many nations
have been destroyed by "average men"?
> (The AVERAGE MAN attempts to get off stage, but
> is prevented by the JUDGE)

Stop! Where do you think you're going? Do you really
think you can escape judgment?

AVERAGE MAN

What's the matter with you, Mister. . . .
> (Giving JUDGE's real name)

What's the big idea, bringing politics into this? A harmless
one-act play, I thought. Why, what you're doing is down-
right vicious!

(Facing the audience)

Ladies and Gentlemen, they have no right to do this to me. I was hired for the part of "Average Man." All of a sudden they pounce on me with that political nonsense. Me! I've been denazified! Hell, no, I've had it. I'm going home!

(Chanting)

Lots and lots I've seen in my days
But never anything like this.

(STAGE MANAGER enters)

STAGE MANAGER

Hold it! Just a moment, Mister. . . .
> (She gives real name of actor playing AVERAGE
> MAN)

You're ruining the entire scene. Look!
> (Shows him copy of script)

It says so right here. Average Man. That's the part you've
been hired for. You're the Average Man.

AVERAGE MAN

Average Man! How dare you! You're insulting my intelli-
gence. Average Man! Some nerve! Don't you realize you're
dealing with a highly educated man?

STAGE MANAGER

Are you completely out of your mind? Of course, I know
who you really are, but tonight you're playing the "Average
Man."
> (Facing the audience)

Will someone kindly hand me a playbill. Mister. . . .

(Giving his real name)
doesn't seem to believe me.

AVERAGE MAN

(Slapping his forehead)
Holy smoke, yes! Forgive me!
(Facing the audience)
Ladies and Gentlemen, this sort of thing is called surrealism. But don't you agree things are getting just a bit too realistic? They make you believe you're just playing a part —just playing, mind you!—and suddenly you find the grease paint of propriety scraped off your face, and you just stand here . . . ! Well, suppose you tell me what you would have done in my place?

JUDGE

Take your place on stage, Average Man!
(AVERAGE MAN does)
So you finally understand that you are to answer *as* the Average Man. Well, then, did you or didn't you denounce the three men?

AVERAGE MAN

Did I or didn't I? Why ask me? I'm just an Average Man, a man of the people. . . .

JUDGE

A man of all the peoples!

AVERAGE MAN

(Meditates upon this for a while, growing increas-
ingly more horrified as the idea takes hold of him.
Then he cries out in horror)
No! No! That can't be true! That isn't true! Never! Never!
That would be too much to bear! If that were true then, as
a German, I tortured Poles and murdered Ukrainians; as a
Pole I expropriated Germans; as a Ukrainian I was a mur-
derous partisan; as an American I pulverized Dresden; as a
Russian I raped and pillaged; as a Frenchman. . . . ! No,
for heaven's sake, no! That's more than I can bear!
(He collapses on the bench)

AVERAGE WOMAN

There you are! I sure know how to spot 'em! That hit home!

JUDGE

Not so fast, my good woman. Now I should like to have the
Average Man tell us who incited him to his actions. Of
course we must remember that we're solely concerned with
the initial precedent. Well, then, who incited the Average
Man to denounce others?

AVERAGE WOMAN

Your Honor, why are you looking at me? I didn't incite
anyone.

JUDGE

Come now, come now.

RAPHAEL

There's no point beating around the bush. Everyone knows it was the Average Woman. In the first story ever told it was "woman." The apple, remember!

GABRIEL

You're not going to drag in that old story!

RAPHAEL

Why not? Who plucked the apple? Who gave it to Adam?

JONAH

Apple, apple! I challenge anyone to show me the passage where it is stated that it was an apple.

MICHAEL

Apple or no apple! What's the difference. A man must pursue his career, must advance in his job. In order to get ahead he must be liked by his superiors. It's always the same story: to improve your family circumstances you must improve your position, and is there a more sure fire way of doing that than by denouncing someone else, and thus getting a better paid job?

AVERAGE WOMAN

(To MICHAEL)

You're still young. Just wait 'til you have children. You don't know how it is when you have kids. How important it is that the man becomes impotent.

(There is much laughter, and she, deeply embar-
rassed, continues)

Important, I mean. My husband simply had to become an
inspector. There were too many mouths to feed. I said that
before, didn't I?

JONAH

But aren't you forgetting that one fine day your children—
for whose sake you pushed your husband—wind up in the
furnace of fire?

AVERAGE WOMAN

Well, they weren't my children.

QUEEN

Only a moment ago you *did* make yourself the spokesman
for all mothers.

AVERAGE WOMAN

I did? Now I'm really getting confused.

MICHAEL

You? Who should get you confused? But me, now take me
for example. First I was responsible for sending Jews to
concentration camps; later I served time in a camp myself.

GABRIEL

Right. The full cycle, my good woman. The chickens come
home to roost. I was a bombardier. I dropped bombs on
London and Coventry, Rotterdam. Later, in Dresden, they
dropped on me.

AVERAGE WOMAN

Well, actually, as far as my own children were concerned, I was very fortunate.

JONAH

We're really not concerned with your personal fate at this moment. The cycle affects each and every one of us. Neither neon lights nor portable TVs offer a solution. Therefore fear, the common fear. . . .

QUEEN

You may stop right there! Things are getting a bit too explicit for comfort.

JUDGE

(To the QUEEN)

You'd like that, wouldn't you? Because now we're getting closer to the major culprit. Who gave the orders? Who did make the weekly paychecks dependent upon blind obedience?

QUEEN

How dare you address me in such fashion. As Judge you are to carry out the laws, but it is I, the Queen, who make them!

(In the back of the house the MERCHANT has risen and is coming down the aisle)

MERCHANT

(He is a prosperous looking, well fed and well
dressed man)
Just a moment, please. Excuse me for interrupting, but
there are a few questions I'd like to ask. It so happens that
I'm very interested in this case. Mind if I come on stage?

JONAH

Not at all. Join us. By all means, do!
(The MERCHANT comes on stage)

MERCHANT

I hope you'll forgive me for this intrusion. I must confess
the proceedings on stage have affected me deeply.

QUEEN

You don't look it.

MERCHANT

Ah, Madame, please, please, you mustn't say that. Does
anything today look the way it should?

55

JONAH

(Impatiently)
You said you wanted to ask some questions.

MERCHANT

Questions! Yes, oh yes of course, questions. I'm a merchant.
At one time I had a beautiful shop. Yes, and I had my own
home, and a wife and two children. I'm saying "had" ad-
visedly, for properly regarded . . . well, how shall I put it?

JUDGE

I take it you're still a merchant.

JONAH

Have you lost your business?

MERCHANT

Well, that's just it. That's what suddenly doesn't . . . well,
frankly, it doesn't seem right to me.
            (With the exception of the JUDGE and MICHAEL
            everyone laughs)

MICHAEL

(To the laughing actors)
Come on, lay off him!

MERCHANT

Must I tell you that the bombs have made me a poor and
lonely man. Just before it occurred to me again. Yes, we'll

never be able to forget completely those days. Sometimes at
night, when sleep doesn't want to come, when you toss and
toss, then, then suddenly I see them again . . . my two
small children, a boy and a girl . . . yes, and my wife, too.
O, she was goodness personified.

(To JUDGE and JONAH)

And now you claim each and everyone of us is responsible
for his own, horrible fate—especially we Germans. Let me
state quite openly and in no uncertain terms that I cannot
accept even the slightest share of the guilt. I never joined
the Party—not an easy thing to do for a man engaged in
trade. As a matter of fact, as a merchant I can tell you that
it isn't always simple to remain honest. It's liable to lead to
bankruptcy and poverty. He . . .

(Pointing to the AVERAGE MAN)

had to provide for his children, therefore he had to make
money. He came to the same conclusion, namely that
honesty isn't always the best policy. In order to provide
properly for his children, he had to curry the favors of his
superiors. We have heard in what fashion.

(Pointing at AVERAGE WOMAN)

The Average Woman only wanted the best for her children;
so she drove them to their deaths.

(Turning to audience)

Ladies and Gentlemen, what sort of world is this! Tell me!
Tell me! Will someone please tell me!

JUDGE

Yes, what sort of world . . . ! Miss. . . .

(Naming the actress playing STAGE MANAGER by
her real name)

please, hand us a different play. We're stuck. This play isn't suitable for our age.
(STAGE MANAGER enters)

STAGE MANAGER

What other play do you have in mind, Mister. . . .
(Gives JUDGE's real name)

JUDGE

Now let's see! Well, for example, we could do "Oedipus." He slew his father and committed incest with his mother . . . though he wasn't aware of the true relationships. Of course one would be entitled to raise the same question over again: what sort of world is this we live in.

MERCHANT

Sounds suitable. "Oedipus." I'm not familiar with the play. But then, I'm afraid I rarely find time to read or to go to the theatre. Is it a modern play?

QUEEN

You mean you haven't discovered that yet?

JONAH

Have all of you gone completely out of your minds! Are you nuts? We're not here to ask questions; they've already been asked. We're here to give answers—*the* answer!

JUDGE

Right! We can't proceed in this fashion.

(Banging gavel)

Order! Order in the Court! Places! Everyone take their places. Yes, the Court cannot permit itself to become involved in digressions. Nothing must interfere with the case under examination. We are here to determine who was responsible for the murder. . . .

GABRIEL

Your Honor, it was not murder, only attempted murder!

JUDGE

The Court stands corrected. Very well, the responsibility for the attempted murder of the three men cast into the furnace of fire. The Court accepts the suggestion of the merchant, Mister. . . .

(To the MERCHANT)

What is your name?

MERCHANT

Tiemann, Your Honor, Ernest Tiemann. Fruits and Vegetables, Wholesale.

JUDGE

The Court accepts the suggestion of Mister Tiemann and extends the scope of this inquiry to determine who bears the primary responsibility for the destruction of Babylon through apocalyptic fire.

MICHAEL

I've been waiting for this point to be raised for a long time.

After all, they can't go on forever pretending that we Germans are the sole culprits.

RAPHAEL

This is Judgment Day we're setting into motion; we mustn't forget our dear neighbors to the East.

JONAH

I object to the term "apocalyptic" fire. I'd hate to see the Lord
            (He motions to the ceiling, and makes a short
            pause for effect)
implicated even before we start our inquiry.

JUDGE

Objection sustained. Let us merely say "fire." This term includes not only the total destruction of entire sections of cities within a few hours, but also the all too familiar phenomenon of death through asphyxiation, suffocation, and burial alive of countless thousands of human beings.

AVERAGE WOMAN

The outcome's a foregone conclusion. You'll arrive at the same stupid result: we're responsible—we who were scared stiff ourselves. What stupidity!

JONAH

Some people just never learn. O yes, I know: the twentieth century can't do wrong. Why can't it be that man is so stupid, so short-sighted? No prejudices, please.

AVERAGE MAN

Oh no, I still say there's a political motive behind all this. The Queen's guilty! She ordered the furnaces built!

QUEEN

(Snapping at the AVERAGE MAN)
You're guilty! You, the average man! I didn't place a single brick, I didn't carry a single log of fire-wood.
(In the meanwhile the three ARCHANGELS have held a quiet huddle. Now GABRIEL steps forward)

```
╔════════════════════════╗
║  SCENE                 ║
║  SEVEN                 ║
╚════════════════════════╝
```

GABRIEL

May I have the floor, Your Honor.

JUDGE

Certainly.

GABRIEL

In the name of the three Archangels I wish to make the following declaration! For several thousand years we, the Archangels, have observed with ever increasing chagrin that those who wield political power have been encroaching upon our duties in shameless fashion. We, the Archangels, have been designated to act as the guardians of nations. . . .

MICHAEL

I, Michael, as guardian angel of Germany. . . .

RAPHAEL

(To MICHAEL)
It's all right. Let *him* speak.

GABRIEL

Yet who prevents us, the appointed leaders of the heavenly
hosts, from guarding the nations so that they won't fall
prey to need and death and despair? The presumptuous,
brazen powers-that-be of the earth! The well-founded suspicion exists among us that the ultimate guilt, the arch-
responsibility for the misfortunes of nations falls upon the
crowned heads. What crass insolence to prevent us, the
Archangels, from exercising our holy and blessed duties.
Power is evil, forever evil. . . .

RAPHAEL

Therefore we move that the inquiry be directed against the
Queen. . . .

QUEEN

Well, this I'm really anxious to hear.

JONAH

I share the Archangel's opinion. The servant merely basks
in his master's glory. When the aristocracy becomes degen-
erate through debauchery and drunkenness, the people turn
into a rabble. Nineveh's sins stank to high heaven when
harlotry and decadence held sway in the halls of the palace;
it was saved when news reached the people that the king
had shed tears of remorse over the sins, and over the prophesied destruction of the city.—Who persisted in sending us
to sea in submarines when the radar- and sonar-equipped
hunters made success and safety impossible?

GABRIEL

Who prolonged the war until my beautiful Dresden collapsed into a heap of rubble and dust?

MICHAEL

And who ordered those decent Amis to drop their damned bombs around the clock?

RAPHAEL

Who chased millions of refugees into the barren countryside? Who gave the orders that were to drive them from the land of their forefathers?

> (A big commotion ensues, in which ALL, with the exception of JONAH and JUDGE, participate. Boos and hooting, shouts and whistling)

ALL

Down with the rulers! Revolution!
> (ALL pointing at the QUEEN)
She did it! She gave the orders!

JUDGE

Enough! That's enough! Order in the Court! Order!
> (When a semblance of order is re-established he turns to the QUEEN)
The people have identified you as the original cause of these excesses.

QUEEN

All right! I identify myself with that. All right! I was the Queen, I ordered the furnaces built, I corrupted the souls of my subjects, I tortured people to death, I tricked them into wars, I ordered saturation bombings of cities! I'm German, English, French, American, Japanese, Russian, Babylonian, Arabian! Do you really believe all that? Do you really believe I could have done all that? Do you honestly believe a human being is capable of all that?

JONAH

Your Honor! I've been saying it all along: the people of every century have never been at a loss for excuses. This is particularly true of our century. In one flash they erase entire cities with their cursed atom bombs; they permit millions of people of another denomination to die in gas chambers, and then they simply tell us: it's monstrous, it's inhuman, therefore it can't be true! But Intercontinental missiles do exist, supersonic sound has been attained, submarines are nuclear-powered.
    (To the audience and the actors on stage)
What sort of delusions do you labor under? Afterwards you tell us something you consider very smart and intelligent. You say it's the inevitable evolution of technology, the evolution of power!
    (To the QUEEN)
And what sort of delusions do *you* labor under? Even though you're the Queen of Babylon tonight—and the Queen of the South—we're not re-enacting an old fairy tale.

QUEEN

Michael, guardian angel of all Germans! I beseech you, protect me from the raving prophet. Can't you offer extenuating circumstances? You're so well versed in the Bible.

MICHAEL

(Thinking for a while)
O yes, this might do.
(To JONAH)
My dear prophet, how does this quotation from the prayers
of your colleague Daniel strike you? "Blessed be the name
of the Lord from everlasting to everlasting, for wisdom and
might are his."

JONAH

But that hardly excuses the lack of wisdom and might in
the human beings.
(To JUDGE)
What is your opinion?

JUDGE

(Rising from his seat, he begins to pace back and
forth agitatedly)
It is terrible! Terrible! Once again the daughter of man is
trying to seduce the angels, just as she did in olden times,
primeval times, when sin was rampant and naked and all
powerful.

MICHAEL

I'm merely quoting from the Holy Scriptures. Now I'm coming to the point: "He changeth the seasons and times, he
removes kings and sets up kings; he gives wisdom to the
wise, and knowledge to those endowed with understanding."

JONAH

So? What is your point?

GABRIEL

(Suddenly greatly agitated)
O, now I understand! Now I understand what Michael's
trying to tell us. It's absurd! No—not absurd, dreadful! I
don't dare say it.

JUDGE

What don't you dare say?

GABRIEL

(Somewhat calmer)
First of all, obviously, it's madness to build furnaces of fire,
to exterminate six million people. . . .

RAPHAEL

To turn untold millions into homeless refugees. . . .

GABRIEL

It is madness to wipe out entire cities merely to win a vic-
tory; to construct atom bombs and to turn the surface of
the globe into a landscape of craters.

QUEEN

Yes, that is true! It was madness, drunkenness!

MICHAEL

In his Revelations, in the eighteenth chapter, John also
mentions drunkenness. Let me think for a moment.—O yes.

Listen: "She is fallen! Mighty Babylon is fallen! She has
become the haunt of demons, and a dungeon for every un-
clean spirit. For after drinking the wine of her immorality
all the heathen have fallen; the kings of the earth have
joined in her idolatry, and the merchants of the earth have
grown rich from excessive luxury!"

MERCHANT

(Moaning aloud, he covers his face with his
hands)
O, my God! O, my God!

MICHAEL

"Then I heard another voice from heaven say, come out of
here, my people, so that you may not share in her sins and
suffer from her plagues!"

AVERAGE WOMAN

Where could we have gone? We had such a beautiful apart-
ment.

AVERAGE MAN

In the end the devil got it anyway.

JUDGE

(To QUEEN)
Do you consider drunkenness an extenuating circumstance?
What nonsense! Who forced you to drink? Who enticed
you to commit these atrocities? But even then it takes two:
the tempter, and the one who permits herself to be
tempted.

RAPHAEL

Perhaps a parable will help. The meaning of an image is at once poetic and divine.

(He approaches the JUDGE with a sly expression)
Imagine a field freshly sewn with seeds. The peasant has completed his task, the seeds sprout and, so to speak, also complete their task. But there's no rain, no sun. Not a very rare occurrence these days. So the crop withers, there is crop failure. The people become needy—tempted, I meant to say, to act evilly, sneaky, viciously. Hunger invariably does that to people. You still remember, don't you? Tell me: who is still indebted to the seed?

JUDGE

Who is still indebted? What did Michael say just before? "He gives wisdom to the wise, and knowledge to those who are endowed with understanding!"

RAPHAEL

Suppose He doesn't give? Who, then, owes the world wisdom and knowledge? Who, then, permits it to lapse into drunkenness?

JONAH

Raphael!!

MICHAEL

(Running to the JUDGE)
It is written in the Book of Job: "Behold: if He destroys,

it cannot be rebuilt; when He shuts up a man, it cannot be reopened; if He sent them forth, they overturn the earth. The misled and the misleader are His!"

JUDGE

What is the meaning of all this? Whom do you mean? Of whom do you speak? Who is this He?

QUEEN

He is the very last to know!

ALL ON STAGE

(Excepting JUDGE and JONAH)
God is guilty! God is guilty! God is guilty!

AVERAGE MAN

Amen!

SCENE
EIGHT

JONAH

God! That is nonsense!

JUDGE

God the guilty one?
        (To the MERCHANT)
Do you believe that, too?

MERCHANT

        (Shrugging shoulders)
I don't really know.—Your Honor, do you find it possible
to believe differently?

JONAH

And the others?
        (Looking at each in turn, he asks each)
You?
        (But all remain silent)
Each of you screamed it at the top of your voices.
        (To JUDGE)
You see, Your Honor, I told you before we even began.
This is the twentieth century, the raving twentieth century!

73

It's incredible. They're already knocking at the gates of hell, but God is guilty! I've known all along it's no use. No use. . . .

JUDGE

(To all except JONAH)
Now, folks, let's be sensible. You folks can't possibly believe that. I plead with you not to believe that. That's impossible.

QUEEN

The trial proved His guilt beyond the shadow of a doubt.

JUDGE

No! I must reject the manner in which evidence has been presented. I can't, I mustn't accept it. Not I. . . .

MERCHANT

Now you're guilty of the same mistake you cautioned others from making: you're revealing prejudices. Please, Your Honor, consider this calmly. Is there any reason why God shouldn't be guilty? As a matter of fact, I've been toying with the idea for quite some time. . . .

JUDGE

You of all people! You who've survived without difficulty?

MERCHANT

What do you mean, without difficulty? Do you think it's such a simple thing to survive?

AVERAGE WOMAN

God is guilty! That's true! True! True! I speak for all the
mothers of the twentieth century! I speak in the name of
all the innocent children who died in the last two wars. I
speak in the name of those who froze to death while fleeing
for their lives—people who were innocent of the atrocities
committed—and whose corpses were thrown into the ditches
along the roads. I speak in the name of all children who,
at an age where they should be playing on sunny play-
grounds, had to face the horrors of their times. I speak in
the name of children who died of hunger and sickness. I
ask, where was the God we were taught to call Father? He
has failed, just as this Court must fail, because the children
aren't here to accuse Him with their emaciated, decayed
bodies, and with eyes hollow from hunger and terror. Can't
you see them? Can you ever rid your memory of that image?
Then join me in my cry: God is guilty! Guilty!

(Wildly sobbing, she collapses on the bench)

MERCHANT

(To the audience)
You who've survived the terror of the bombing raids, give
us the remaining wretches! Give them to me! I haven't any
any more. He let them perish in the flames. Burnt alive,
helplessly stuck in molten asphalt. O curses! Curses! Curses!

JONAH

(To JUDGE)
That's the raving mad twentieth century.

QUEEN

(Having overheard this last remark)
No! It's the voice of the rabble that must be ruled with furnaces of fire, that must be forced to pray to idols because they enslave without mercy! I was obliged to tame wild beasts! Who dares call me a sinner because I used a whip! Seat yourself upon a throne; from up high you get to know mankind. Every village, every hamlet, is chock full of whores and thieves and drunkards. For a tiny reward brother betrays brother. Only fire and sword keep them in line! Build more furnaces!

(Turning to the audience)
It is for you that I need them! While fighting men of all nations were locked in mortal combat, while prisoners of war suffered privations, where were you? Where were you when millions were gassed? Counting profits, and concerned with your pleasures and comforts only.

(To the MERCHANT)
You mongrel dog! I know all about you! You built yourself a beautiful store to make money. In the rubble they found human remains. And twenty years ago, on the very same spot, stood the store of David Mayer, later gassed at Auschwitz!

(To the audience)
Where twenty years ago you demolished the apartments of Jews and desecrated their synagogues and beat them, you now have your neon signs, you mongrels, and when Christmas comes, one tree standing next to another. Peace on earth! Hahaha . . . ! Just let me hold the reins once more . . . !

(Laughing shrilly, hysterically, she breaks down, and JONAH leads her to the bench)

JONAH

Calm yourself, please, calm yourself.

AVERAGE MAN

Your Honor, may I have the floor!

JUDGE

(Wearily)
If you must, go ahead.

AVERAGE MAN

Look at me, gentlemen, as I stand before you. A man? The crowning glory of the creation? Haha! A wreck! I'm an average man, the man of the street. No, the man *in* the street. Do you know what that means? Goose stepping! Goose stepping for a dozen years. Goose stepping, goose stepping, goose stepping. I've suffered hunger and thirst and the fear of death. I was a man broken in body and spirit when they discharged me before the end of the war. The First War, that is. Did the fatherland grant me my well-earned rest? Like that gentleman here. . . .
(Pointing at the MERCHANT)
I, too, was dealt harsh blows in my old age. The Second War robbed me of my two sons. My beloved wife died from grief and privations, for we were driven from the home of our fathers. Our daughter, a lovely, pale, angelic little girl, died of typhoid. She was to have been the joy and solace of our old age. I ask you, can any man have sinned so terribly that he must bear such a burden?

(Pausing briefly, then)

You're all silent, all of you, even the Archangels. With my
last ounce of strength I dragged myself here, for only the
burning desire to get even keeps me going.

(To JUDGE)

Your Honor! If this court is just, you must pronounce a
just sentence. If you can locate the God whom I lost in the
course of two wars, condemn Him, as I am condemned, to
lead the life of man on earth. Let Him wander about, as I
must wander about, without a home to rest His weary head.
Let Him feel the pain, as I feel the pain, of having lost His
son. Let Him suffer, as I had to suffer, hunger and thirst
and the fear of death. Then, perhaps, in future centuries,
He will govern more wisely. . . .

MERCHANT

(Eagerly shaking the AVERAGE MAN's hand)

Your faith is not unique. I know how it is. . . .

JONAH

You see, Your Honor, the twentieth century. I warned you
against having anything to do with these people.

JUDGE

I must admit it is highly irregular for a witness to pronounce
sentence. However, the Court will take cognizance of his
remarks. I'm beginning to realize myself that the evidence
against the unknown defendant is overwhelming.

QUEEN

If anyone, by virtue of rank and position, is entitled to pronounce judgment, it is I. Except you, of course, Your Honor.

(Slightly inclines her head to JUDGE)

A short while ago, in this very room, grave accusations have been levelled against me. No one is happier than I to find that the true circumstances have been brought into the open. The higher one's position, the more painful the fall, if fall one must. We have heard the accusations of the father, the accusations of the mother. What are they compared to my own sufferings? The mother lost her children, the father his family and home. But I, a sovereign, lost an entire country. My capital, rich, happy, golden Babylon, collapsed into rubble and dust within one hour. Once the rulers of the earth paid me homage; here I must suffer accusations of harlotry and wickedness. Yes, I ordered the furnaces built! It had to be! I was compelled to do it! My position demands that I lead my people, give them laws to preserve order among them, for man left to himself is chaos. In order to enforce the laws I had to be severe. I was forced to kill in order to preserve life. Who created man in such fashion that only the threat of death and terror make him manageable? God! Who arranged the world in such fashion that kings must commit greater sins than other mortals? God! Who forces us to keep our nations alive by leading them up to the altar of war, to be bled white? God! Who transforms the clearcut actions of the princes into terrible ambiguity? God! Who transforms our crowns of gold into crowns of thorns? There is only one answer, though everyone seems wary to pronounce it. Only one verdict is possible: God must become king of kings! He must be forced to make laws for man! He must wear the crown of thorns, and from a place of high honor he must be thrust into damnation. This I say, in the name of those who ever wore a crown!

JUDGE

(After a brief silence)
Archangels! You have heard the accusations. I command you to inform God of the verdict. How shall we phrase it?

AVERAGE MAN

God shall become a human being, a wanderer on earth, deprived of his rights, homeless, hungry, thirsty, in constant fear of death.

AVERAGE WOMAN

He shall be born to a woman, somewhere along a country road, and the moans of the poor creature shall ring in His ears day and night. He shall be surrounded by the feeble, the sick, the filthy, by people bearing the marks of leprosy. Rotting corpses shall bar His path. He shall know what it means to die. He, himself, shall die!

AVERAGE MAN

And lose a son, and suffer the agonies of fatherhood.

QUEEN

And when at last He dies, He shall be disgraced and ridiculed.

JUDGE

Do you consider this sentence to be just and proper? Does no one object?

JONAH

Of course not.

JUDGE

(Touching each as he calls his name)
Michael! Gabriel! Raphael! You, you the spokesmen of God, what say you?
(All three shake their heads in silence)
Go then! Inform Him of the verdict rendered by a tortured humanity.

GABRIEL

I, Gabriel, shall go to a country ruled by cruel, parasitic men, a divided land occupied by a foreign power. I shall go to a virgin named Mary. She shall bring God into the world, under suspicion of shame—and as a Jew!

MICHAEL

I, Michael, shall order the Heavenly Hosts to let Him walk the earth unprotected. When He falls to His knees, when the curse of being a man sends sweat dripping from His brow like drops of blood, I shall grant Him sufficient strength only that He may go on suffering, shall console Him as He consoled the faithful, putting them off with promises so that they can bear more suffering.

RAPHAEL

I, Raphael, shall be present when He sinks into death, and I shall stand by His grave and be the horror's holiest witness that God is dead!

JUDGE

O, what have I done! I condemned God! Never again shall I sit in Judgment. Human beings may rightfully fear my decisions.

(To the ARCHANGELS)

I shall go with you. I can no longer be judge!

(He and the ARCHANGELS exit. JONAH now takes the JUDGE's place in center stage, while all the other actors move to the opposite side of the stage)

JONAH

(After a lengthy pause)

What do you think you really have accomplished, people of the twentieth century? Do you think you have done something particularly bold, have made a new discovery?— It is just a rediscovery! We could continue in modern fashion now, show you something very appropriate by means of a projector and a movie screen. It would probably be as effective as the before-mentioned *mene tekel*, particularly if we employed the creations of top artists—Dürer's woodcut of the Birth of Christ, for example, and Grunewald's painting of the Crucifixion. But good taste prevents us from showing you the actual execution of the verdict. You know that it was carried out, and you know in what fashion. We merely wish to remind you of it.

(He pauses briefly)

There is little else for us up here on stage to do, since it is a reasonable assumption that you, to a certain degree, are somewhat involved in your own thoughts.

(Again pauses briefly)

As you might have noticed, all the remaining actors have felt that something has transpired, and for that reason they

83

have changed places. Miss. . . .

> (He names actress playing QUEEN by her real
> name)

Will you kindly tell us what you're trying to indicate by
this change of place?

QUEEN

Simply this: a human being can be anything in his or her
lifetime, enact one role or another. Man only has to make
the proper decision.

> (Brief pause)

Now we're no longer Babylonians, but the people of Nineveh and Sheba who, it was prophesied, will rise with the
men of this generation at the Judgment, and no sign will be
given it but the Sign of Jonah.

AVERAGE WOMAN

Therefore we had to omit the Sign of the Manger and the
Sign of the Cross.

AVERAGE MAN

But the earth is filled with suffering mothers. . . .

MERCHANT

And crosses, so many crosses.

QUEEN

But the reawakening of half-forgotten memories holds
hardly enough promise for the men of this generation.

> (The STAGE MANAGER enters)

Which is the reason why the author has inserted a motto
at the head of this script:
>   (She reads)
"The Queen of the South will rise with the men of this
generation. . . .
>   (Pointing at the MERCHANT)
at the Judgment and will condemn them, for she came
from the very ends of the earth to listen to Solomon's wisdom, and there is more than Solomon here! Men of
Nineveh will rise with the men of this generation
>   (Pointing at MERCHANT again)
at the Judgment and will condemn it, for they repented at
Jonah's preaching, and there is more than Jonah here!"

JONAH

>   (To the AVERAGE MAN and WOMAN who are stand-
>   ing together)
Yes, yes, Nineveh! Those were wonderful days when our
city was still undamaged. I came to you, and for three
days I wandered through your beautiful streets and squares,
and admired the mighty edifices and the neat little homes,
for never before had I been in Berlin—Nineveh, I meant
to say! And then I told you how God had filled me with
fear upon fear while I was at sea, until finally I was lost in
the terrible blackness inside the whale.

AVERAGE WOMAN

And you asked, "do you love your city?"

AVERAGE MAN

And we said, "yes, from the bottom of our hearts."

AVERAGE WOMAN

And then you asked, "do you love your children?"

AVERAGE MAN

And we said . . .

MERCHANT

(Interrupts, deeply moved)
. . . more than anything in the world!

AVERAGE WOMAN

And then you said, "weep for your city, for there are only forty more days left, and Nineveh will be destroyed."

QUEEN

And this news reached the palace. You told us of your own godless ways, and how you had to pass through hell before returning to God. So I ordered . . .

AVERAGE MAN

. . . everyone to join in a fast . . .

AVERAGE WOMAN

. . . and we tore our luxurious gowns and sprinkled ashes on our heads, for we knew the end was near.

AVERAGE MAN

Yes, it was a stern ordinance.

QUEEN

My husband, the king, and I abandoned all pride and vanity and discarded our crowns, for we knew we were in the wrong, and that Jonah was right.

JONAH

For everything which tonight was brought before the bar of justice is the fruit of human viciousness. Man is always threatened by his fellow man.

AVERAGE MAN

And by his own guilt.

MERCHANT

(To QUEEN)

Then tell me, how did you manage to banish the threats inherent in man? For your city was spared, wasn't it?

AVERAGE MAN

O yes, it was spared. Nineveh the beautiful, she was spared. And Nineveh became even more beautiful, for the people repented and led godfearing lives. "God bless our Nineveh," was the friendly greeting from friendly lips. And where once had stood the furnaces of fire, no one, even secretly, rebuilt them. And where once atrocities had been committed, no colored lights and decorations were permitted to camouflage these places of horrible, but sobering memories.

MERCHANT

You mean neon lights and Christmas trees?

AVERAGE MAN

If that's the way you like to interpret it, for yourself and for your country, it's all right with me. We searched ourselves . . .

MERCHANT

(To QUEEN)
How did it occur to you to proclaim the saving ordinance?

QUEEN

I wish I could answer you that past experiences brought it about. But unfortunately man quickly forgets past experiences. Then it is well to take advice from proper sources. I had heard of the wisdom of Solomon, that powerful king of noble lineage. So I travelled across the desert, to learn from his wisdom, for wisdom is the essential requisite for a ruler.

MERCHANT

And what did you learn?

QUEEN

The wisdom of Solomon, even then, a thousand years before the birth of the Saviour, was something so unique it was well worth crossing the great desert to hear it; even in those days when the world was foolish and hostile and lengthy travel dangerous. Solomon alone was wise, for he stood in awe of God.

MERCHANT

He stood in awe of God?

AVERAGE MAN

The reason Nineveh was saved.

AVERAGE MAN

We knew that man is always in the wrong before God.

MERCHANT

Then what am I to do? On the site where my shop stands today human remains were found, and before that, other human beings suffered torture and shame and fear.

JONAH

Condemn yourself, then God will acquit you.

QUEEN

As the Judge condemned himself.

MERCHANT

The Judge . . .?
        (Looking at everyone questioningly)

JONAH

He administered the law in place of God.

MERCHANT

God condemned God! And we, we! accused Him! O, never again, never!
     (The JUDGE enters)

JUDGE

Then, after all, it was not in vain.

MERCHANT

No, it was not in vain. Let me assure you, it was not in vain!

JONAH

     (To the audience)
For one man it was not in vain. What about you, ladies and gentlemen?

MAN IN THE AUDIENCE

Right you are, you up there! It was not in vain!
     (The ARCHANGELS return)

MICHAEL

Ah, Mister Trick. Well, why don't you come up here? Join us! We're almost finished.

RAPHAEL

(Pointing at the MAN IN THE AUDIENCE)
He is also a trick.

GABRIEL

One is almost tempted to say that our fate is a trick of God,
to help us find the truth.

JONAH

(To audience)
Well, ladies and gentlemen, the fear of the Lord is the
beginning of wisdom. A beginning, a terrible beginning perhaps, but better than none. If you enjoyed the tricks up
here on stage, then please recommend our playlet to your
friends . . . and enemies. You have a pretty good idea
what shape the world is in. There is room for quite a few
improvements. Or must we suffocate once more in a submarine? Our future lives will give the answer.

        (pointing at the side where the accusers of God
        had stood)
One way—

        (pointing at the side where the people of Nineveh
        had stood)
or the other. I wish you a pleasant way home. Do not
elbow your way to the exit. There is no need to rush. No
bombs will fall . . . tonight!

THE END